track and field
running & field events

Consultant

Harvey Greer, asst. track coach
University of Kansas
Lawrence,
Kansas

Demonstrators

Members of the University of
Kansas Track and Field Team

published by:
The Athletic Institute
Merchandise Mart, Chicago

*A not-for-profit organization
devoted to the advancement of
athletics, physical education
and recreation.*

Robert G. Bluth, Editor

**Library of Congress
Catalog Card Number 79-109498**

**"Sports Techniques" Series
SBN 87670-050-4**

Published by The Athletic Institute
Chicago, Illinois 60654

Foreword

The SPORTS TECHNIQUES SERIES is but one item in a comprehensive list of sports instructional aids which are made available by The Athletic Institute. This book is part of a master plan which seeks to make the benefits of athletics, physical education and recreation available to everyone.

The Athletic Institute is a not-for-profit organization devoted to the advancement of athletics, physical education and recreation. The Institute believes that participation in athletics and recreation has benefits of inestimable value to the individual and to the community.

The nature and scope of the many Institute programs are determined by a *Professional Advisory Committee,* whose members are noted for their outstanding knowledge, experience and ability in the fields of athletics, physical education and recreation.

The Institute believes that through this book the reader will become a better performer, skilled in the fundamentals of this fine sport. Knowledge and the practice necessary to mold knowledge into playing ability are the keys to real enjoyment in playing any game or sport.

The sport of track and field aids in the development of motor skill, flexibility, agility and endurance as well as providing enjoyable recreation.

Donald E. Bushore
Executive Director
The Athletic Institute

Introduction

The purpose of this book is to give the reader an understanding of the fundamentals of track and field. It is not intended to be a scientific analysis of techniques, nor does it make an attempt to delve deeply into the finer points of each event. It is written for the beginning coach and athlete with the belief that if the individual learns to perform his event correctly during the primary stages of his athletic career, his opportunities for success and complete development will be greatly increased.

Harvey Greer

Table of Contents

Table of Contents (Continued)

the start

Success in sprint events depends to a great extent on natural speed and reaction time.

Regardless of how fast a sprinter might be, he may lose valuable time because of a poor start. Usually, the start is one variable which the sprinter may improve upon greatly.

The Starting Blocks

Standard *starting blocks* afford the sprinter the possibility of a strong, fast start.

Starting blocks vary as to styling and material, but most generally are of one-piece construction and are adjustable to personal desires and specifications of the performer.

Become acquainted with a variety of starting blocks used at the various meets in which you may perform.

1. STANDARD STARTING BLOCKS USUALLY ARE OF ONE-PIECE CONSTRUCTION AND ARE ADJUSTABLE TO PERSONAL REQUIREMENTS.

2. BECOME FAMILIAR WITH THE COMMON TYPES OF BLOCKS WHICH YOU MAY BE CALLED UPON TO USE.

Sprint Start Techniques

Make the necessary starting block adjustments suited to your starting style and comfort.

First call is **"Runners, Stand at Your Blocks"** or a command of a similar nature.

"Runners Go to Your Marks"

Upon this command from the starter, stand in front of your blocks with the toe of the left foot 12 to 18 inches behind the starting line and with the toe of the right foot some four to six inches behind the heel of the left foot. Exact placement of the feet varies with individuals.

Lower the right knee to the ground next to the left foot. From this position, lean forward and place your hands behind the starting line. The inside of the left elbow barely touches the left knee. Hands are spread a shoulder's width apart with the fingers and thumb touching the ground. Thumb and index finger are placed behind the starting line with remaining fingers bunched in back of the index finger. Fingers and thumb form a supporting arch.

Adjust feet in the starting blocks and focus your eyes downward or on a spot a few feet in front of you. Most of the body weight is to the back and on the right knee.

1. **STAND IN FRONT OF BLOCKS WITH LEFT FOOT 12 TO 18 INCHES BEHIND THE STARTING LINE AND RIGHT FOOT SLIGHTLY BEHIND HEEL OF LEFT FOOT.**

2. **LOWER RIGHT KNEE TO GROUND NEXT TO LEFT FOOT. LEAN FORWARD AND PLACE HANDS BEHIND STARTING LINE. HANDS SHOULDER'S WIDTH APART. FINGERS AND THUMB FORM SUPPORTING ARCH.**

3. **WITH FEET INSERTED IN STARTING BLOCKS, MAKE SLIGHT ADJUSTMENTS.**

4. **FOCUS EYES DOWNWARD OR ON A SPOT A FEW FEET IN FRONT.**

"Set"

After this command, raise your hips approximately shoulder high to shift weight over your hands. Take a deep breath. The foreleg portion of the right leg should be nearly parallel with the ground. The left knee is bent at a 90-degree angle.

Focus your eyes some eight to ten yards down the track. Concentrate only on the start. Block out actions of competitors and spectators in the stands.

5. **RAISE HIPS TO SHOULDER HEIGHT, SHIFTING WEIGHT OVER HANDS. TAKE DEEP BREATH.**

6. **RIGHT FORELEG NEARLY PARALLEL WITH GROUND, LEFT KNEE BENT AT 90-DEGREE ANGLE.**

7. **FOCUS EYES 8 TO 10 YARDS DOWN TRACK CONCENTRATE FULLY ON START.**

The Gun ("Go")

React instantly to the firing of the gun by exhaling forcefully and driving from the blocks with both legs.

The left arm projects forward while the right knee drives forward and slightly upward. The left leg exerts tremendous pressure against the front block to extend fully off the block.

Many beginning sprinters often fail to drive the right leg and left arm forward.

First stride from the blocks should be as long as can be controlled effectively. Generally this means that the right foot will land from four to 16 inches in front of the starting line. Eyes are focused about three to five yards in front.

Keep the angle of the body low to the ground for the first 10 to 15 yards. The first strides are shorter, but not choppy. The natural, forward lean of the body will cause the stride to be shorter until the normal, upright position is achieved.

Drive arms vigorously for balance and keep knees high. Learn to relax. By relaxing, you run with longer strides resulting in better times.

8. **AT GUN, EXPLODE FROM BLOCKS BY EXHALING FORCEFULLY, PROJECTING THE LEFT ARM FORWARD AND DRIVING FORWARD WITH BOTH LEGS.**

9. **DRIVE LEFT LEG OFF BLOCK TO FULL EXTENSION. DRIVE FORWARD, NOT UP. FIRST STRIDES AS LONG AS CAN BE CONTROLLED. ON FIRST STRIDE, RIGHT FOOT LANDS 4 TO 16 INCHES FROM THE STARTING LINE.**

10. ANGLE BODY FORWARD AND LOW TO THE GROUND FOR FIRST 10 TO 15 YARDS. AS ONE ARM PROJECTS FORWARD TOWARD THE FINISH LINE AND PARALLEL WITH GROUND, THE OPPOSITE ARM AND HAND SWING BACK TO A HEIGHT EVEN WITH HIP.

11. DRIVE ARMS VIGOROUSLY TO AID BALANCE AND RUN WITH KNEES HIGH.

12. RUN RELAXED. ELONGATE STRIDE ONCE NATURAL, UPRIGHT RUNNING POSITION IS ACHIEVED.

The "Elongated" Start

Both coach and runner should realize that no two sprinters are exactly alike, therefore each may prefer one style to others. Certainly, the foregoing starting fundamentals are most basic, yet some phases of the start allow for personal preference.

The *"Elongated" Start* is most natural to many sprinters. Front and back blocks are spaced approximately 24 to 30 inches apart. Experiment to find the exact placement which affords the most comfort and power. Once you have found the desired block positions, mark these spots for future reference.

The "Bunch" Start

Some sprinters prefer to start from blocks spaced more closely together.

In the *"Bunch" Start,* the blocks are spaced about six to 12 inches apart.

Regardless of how far you prefer to start, your success in starting depends greatly upon reaction time, strength and application of basic techniques.

Practice the start often to fully develop your starting capability.

The "Standing" Sprint Start

Recently, considerable interest has been shown in the possibility that a standing start in sprint and hurdle events may be more effective than the traditional sprint (crouch) start.

Highly publicized experiments in South Africa coupled with supporting statements by a few leading U.S. coaches are influencing more sprinters to attempt the standing start.

The question becomes, which start allows the runner to achieve the optimum trunk position for accelerating out of the blocks? The crouch starter begins lower than the level of the optimum position because he must keep his hands on the ground. The standing starter starts higher than the optimum position to keep from extending over the starting line.

During the first stride, can the standing starter lower his body to the optimum position more quickly than could he raise his body to that position from a crouched start? Whatever starting style allows a sprinter to reach the optimum trunk position fastest for acceleration out of the blocks, would seem best for him to use. To date, conclusive evidence does not show that one style is superior to the other for the majority of sprinters.

Start for Middle Distance and Long Distance Runs

Sprints are those races up to and including the 440-yard dash. Some coaches prefer to think of the 440 as a middle distance race, especially at the high school level since many runners lack the physical capability to run the race completely as a sprint. Nevertheless, the sprint start is used for the 440 as it is for races of less distance.

The 880-yard run is truly a middle distance race in which the runner may wish to use a modified sprint start or a standing start.

A runner choosing to use blocks for the 880 is not required to explode out of the blocks to the extent that the sprinter must. By using blocks, the runner wants to make sure that his start is smooth and clean.

The standing start is used for distances of a mile and longer. For races of these distances, the standing start is preferred because it requires considerably less energy. Furthermore, the start is of lesser importance for longer races than for a sprint.

How a runner starts from a standing position is almost wholly a matter of personal preference. Some runners prefer to lean slightly forward at the waist with one foot in back of the other, while others feel more comfortable and get better results by crouching more forward.

This is not to say that the start for a long distance run is not important. Quite the contrary, a good start often means a good position relative to the rest of the field which eventually may prove to be an important factor in winning.

sprinting and distance running

Coaches and athletes should be familiar with fundamental running movements. Running form is a very individual matter.

Because of individual differences in physical make-up, the form of one runner is slightly different from that of another. Therefore, running form can be described only in general terms.

Body Angle When Running

Once a steady running speed is attained, the *body angle* tends toward the perpendicular. A slight forward lean may be necessary when running into a wind—the stronger the wind the greater the lean. Most runners, from sprints to the marathon, use a very erect body carriage, once a steady speed is achieved. When the rate of acceleration in sprinting is greatest, the forward lean also must be at its greatest. The sprinter has a tremendous forward lean at the start of his run. From the instant he starts to the point at which he reaches top speed, his rate of acceleration gradually diminishes although his speed is increasing. The degree of forward lean decreases as top speed is approached. At top speed, in the absence of wind resistance, there would be no lean at all. However, a runner travelling some 20-odd miles per hour at top speed on a perfectly calm and windless day will create his own wind resistance. He requires a slight forward lean to offset the resistance but not much.

1. FORWARD LEAN GREATEST WHEN ACCELERATING.

2. ONCE RUNNING SPEED IS ACHIEVED, BODY ANGLE TENDS TOWARD THE PERPENDICULAR.

3. SLIGHT FORWARD LEAN MAY BE NECESSARY WHEN RUNNING INTO WIND.

Head Position

The head is directed to the front, bent neither forward nor backward and held in natural alignment with the body. If individual considerations cause you to run with your head high because it is uncomfortable any other way, you should be permitted to do so providing it does not cause you to lean backward or otherwise decrease your rate of forward progress.

1. RUN WITH HEAD DIRECTED TO THE FRONT, BENT NEITHER FORWARD NOR BACKWARD.

2. INDIVIDUAL PREFERENCE MAY PERMIT SLIGHT CHANGE IN HEAD POSITION PROVIDING FORWARD PROGRESS IS NOT AFFECTED.

Arm Action

Arm action plays a balancing role in running. As the right leg strides forward, the right shoulder moves back and the left shoulder, forward. The left arm comes forward, around the body, while the right arm moves back. As the left leg comes forward, the movement of the arms is reversed.

Arm action must be around the body in a forward direction and must not hinder the running progression. The lower arm comes forward with each step. Higher arm action is faster than lower arm action. Higher arm action is usually associated with faster leg action although the legs actually lead the arms. However, at the finish of the race when the legs are weak from fatigue, the arms are used to drive the legs faster. Action and reaction of the legs and arms are interchangeable.

The arm action must be a natural movement, devoid of unnatural tension. If the arms get tired quickly or ache while running, perhaps they are being held in an unnatural position or are subjected to unnecessary tension.

The hands are held in a relaxed "cup" position, not in a tight fist.

1. **AS THE RIGHT LEG STRIDES FORWARD, LEFT ARM COMES FORWARD AND AROUND BODY WHILE RIGHT ARM MOVES BACK.**

2. **SEQUENCE IS REVERSED WHEN LEFT LEG STRIDES FORWARD. HIGHER ARM ACTION FASTER THAN LOWER ARM ACTION.**

3. ARM ACTION IS A NATURAL MOVEMENT, DEVOID OF TENSION.

4. HANDS HELD IN RELAXED, "CUP" POSITION.

Leg Action

Leg action propels the body forward.

The forward foot contacts the track directly under the body's projected center of gravity. The knee of the forward leg is bent at the moment of contact. The outer edge of the ball of the foot makes first contact with the track. Immediately thereafter the heel touches the track. Any muscular effort to prevent the heel from touching the track is positively unnatural and should be discouraged.

Power should be applied over the greatest possible foot area to achieve maximum acceleration—thus if the heel does not touch the track for at least an **instant** when running at any distance, then power cannot be applied over the greatest possible area to achieve maximum acceleration.

During the instant the foot is flat upon the track, it bears the runner's full weight, and the body rides smoothly forward for the next stride. Actually, the foot has come to a complete stop for an instant. As the body weight continues to ride forward over the bent knee, the heel first is lifted and then, as the knee is fully extended (straightened), the toe leaves the track for the next stride. Briefly, the action of the foot is ball, heel, ball in landing and leaving the track.

1. FORWARD FOOT CONTACTS TRACK DIRECTLY UNDER PROJECTED CENTER OF GRAVITY.

2. OUTER EDGE OF BALL OF FOOT MAKES FIRST CONTACT FOLLOWED INSTANTLY BY HEEL.

   ATTEMPTING TO PREVENT HEEL FROM CONTACTING TRACK IF ONLY SLIGHTLY IS UNNATURAL.

3. HEEL CONTACT HELPS TO PROVIDE MAXIMUM LEVERAGE FOR ACCELERATION.

4. KNEE IS BENT UPON CONTACT.

5. SEQUENCE OF FOOT ACTION IS "BALL, HEEL, BALL."

Stride Length

Quite often, *stride length* is misunderstood. The slower the speed of the run, the shorter the stride length should be. The faster the run, the longer the stride.

A runner takes the longest stride when sprinting and decreases the stride length when running more slowly. Sprinters take the longest strides and marathon runners, the shortest.

Longer strides are faster but require far more energy. A sprinter is not concerned primarily with conservation of energy, therefore uses the longer, faster but less economical long stride.

As the racing distance increases, economy of effort becomes more important. Athletes naturally adjust the stride length accordingly. Two short strides carry the runner farther than one long stride and they require far less energy.

In races longer than the sprints, wherein economy of stride motion is a prime consideration, a runner should take a natural step—not exaggerated, not short, but a natural step in keeping with maximum economy of effort for the speed required.

1. THE SLOWER THE SPEED OF RUN, THE SHORTER THE STRIDE.

2. CONVERSELY, THE FASTER THE RUN, THE LONGER THE STRIDE.

3. LONGER STRIDES REQUIRE MORE ENERGY. IN DISTANCE RACES WHERE ECONOMY OF ENERGY IS IMPORTANT, SHORTER STRIDES SHOULD BE TAKEN.

HOWEVER, TAKE A NATURAL STEP, NOT AN EXAGGERATED SHORT STEP.

the hurdles

A *hurdle race* is a sprint to the first hurdle, a sprint between hurdles and a sprint to the tape. Between sprints the basic factor to success is form over the hurdle. A hurdle must be cleared with as little loss of speed as possible.

The Start

As in the case of the sprint, the start for the hurdles is most important and something which should be practiced continuously.

Most hurdlers take seven or eight strides to the first high hurdle, 10 strides to the first low hurdle and 21 to 23 strides to the first intermediate hurdle.

The start is basically that of a sprint start except that the high hurdler reaches a more upright running position sooner than a sprinter or a hurdler in a low or intermediate hurdle race.

1. PRACTICE HURDLE START OFTEN.

2. NUMBER OF STRIDES TO FIRST HIGH HURDLE IS 7 OR 8; TO THE FIRST LOW HURDLE, 10 STRIDES; TO THE FIRST INTERMEDIATE HURDLE, 21 TO 23 STRIDES.

3. ALL SPRINT START TECHNIQUES APPLY EXCEPT THAT THE HIGH HURDLER ACHIEVES UPRIGHT, RUNNING POSITION SOONER.

Learning to Hurdle

Some beginning hurdlers may be somewhat apprehensive about approaching and jumping over a hurdle.

Often these prospective hurdlers find comfort in walking over a low hurdle a number of times before attempting the jump.

Hurdling Form

In stepping over a hurdle, stand about two feet from the face. Be certain to lift the lead knee so the leg goes straight over the hurdle. Bring the trailing leg through in a flat position and pull it quickly across the hurdle.

After walking over the hurdle 10 to 15 times, try running a series of hurdles using the form learned in walking over them.

Run over the hurdles for a short period, then practice walking over them once again.

Through this simple drill, surprising success may be achieved.

Hurdling Techniques

Lifting the lead knee straight up is most fundamental to hurdling success. This is not to say that the leg is held straight when going over the hurdle, only that the vertical lift of the knee should be in a straight line to the direction of the run. Actually, the front foot is kicked straight at the hurdle. Do not swing the lead leg. Throwing the front leg out to the side causes loss of distance and balance.

Most right-handed hurdlers prefer to lead with the left leg.

If this is not comfortable for you, try leading with the right leg. However, leading with the left leg has an advantage over leading with the right when running hurdles on a curve.

Usually, the takeoff point is 6½ to seven feet from the hurdle. When leading with the left leg over a hurdle, reach in front with the right arm toward the left foot. While the right arm goes forward, the left arm comes back so that the left hand is positioned outside the left hip. Reverse this action when leading with the right leg. This position provides good balance and the chance to cross the hurdle in proper position to continue the sprint. In a driving motion, the body bends over the lead leg.

While going over the hurdle, the back leg lays flat with toes pointing out to the side, not downward. Pull the trailing leg across the hurdle as quickly as possible. A strong, initial kick with the lead leg will help pull the back leg through faster.

By bringing the trailing leg through with good knee action, the first step after the hurdle is as long as possible. Also, by such action, the foot will land in front of the body in the direction of the run.

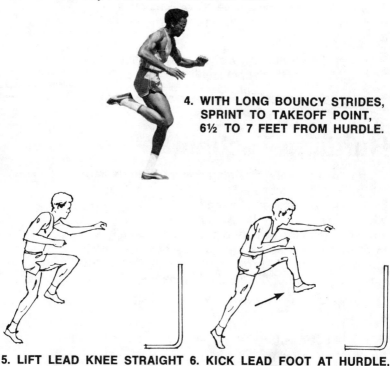

4. WITH LONG BOUNCY STRIDES, SPRINT TO TAKEOFF POINT, 6½ TO 7 FEET FROM HURDLE.

5. LIFT LEAD KNEE STRAIGHT TO DIRECTION OF RUN.

6. KICK LEAD FOOT AT HURDLE, LEAN FORWARD AND PROJECT OPPOSITE ARM TOWARD LEAD FOOT AS REAR FOOT LEAVES GROUND.

7. BODY BENDS OVER LEAD LEG IN DRIVING MOTION, BACK LEG LAYS FLAT WITH TOES POINTING OUT TO SIDE.

8. PULL TRAILING LEG ACROSS HURDLE QUICKLY BY STRONG, INITIAL KICK WITH LEAD LEG. BRING TRAILING LEG THROUGH WITH HIGH KNEE ACTION.

9. FIRST STRIDE AFTER HURDLE SHOULD BE AS LONG AS POSSIBLE.

Note: The primary difference in running the high hurdles and low hurdles involves body angle.

When running the low hurdles, the forward lean is not as pronounced nor is the stretching of the lead arm.

A low hurdle race is essentially a sprint. In fact, some of the best low hurdlers are sprinters as well.

Sprinting Between Hurdles

Good hurdlers take only three strides between high hurdles, seven strides between low hurdles and 15 to 17 strides between intermediate hurdles. It is important to start well on the first hurdle, run with knees high and take an elongated stride after coming off each hurdle.

The only way to lengthen the stride is to lift the knees higher with exaggerated arm action.

After a hurdle, the first two steps of a beginning hurdler are usually shorter than the third while the first two steps of an advanced hurdler will be slightly longer than the third. **Work on lengthening the first stride after each hurdle.**

10. TAKE 3 STRIDES BETWEEN EACH HIGH HURDLE, 7 STRIDES BETWEEN EACH LOW HURDLE AND 15 TO 17 STRIDES BETWEEN EACH INTERMEDIATE HURDLE.

11. START WELL ON FIRST HURDLE, RUN WITH KNEES HIGH, TAKE ELONGATED STRIDE COMING OFF EACH HURDLE. EXAGGERATE ARM ACTION FOR LONG STRIDE.

Tips for Beginning Hurdlers

If you have trouble reaching each hurdle in the maximum number of strides suggested, place the hurdles closer together.

Gradually, space the hurdles farther apart as you elongate your stride to cover more distance but run with the same number of strides. Ultimately, you will reach the level of proficiency allowing you to space each hurdle at the official distance.

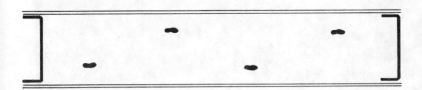

Portions of the instructional material presented in this book were submitted by Fred Wilt, author of the book—*Track in Theory and Technique,* published by the Asian Track and Field Coaches Assn.

The Athletic Institute is most grateful to the author and publisher for permission to use this material.

the relay

Apart from starting, running and finishing, a team relay race involves one further variable, that of exchanging a baton.

The baton exchange within the passing zone with runners running at top speed is one of the most exciting maneuvers in all sports.

The Sprint Baton Pass

Starting a Sprint Relay

All basic sprint start techniques apply when starting a sprint relay.

Hold the baton with **four fingers** while resting the thumb and knuckles behind the starting line.

As you come away from the starting line at the gun, close the thumb around the baton.

With the baton in the **right hand,** the lead runner passes the baton to the **left hand** of the second runner. The second runner passes to the **right hand** of the third runner who in turn passes to the **left hand** of the anchor man.

If starting with the baton in the **left hand,** the first pass is to the **right hand** of the second runner. The second runner passes to the **left hand** of the third man who passes to the **right hand** of the last runner.

In some races it may be more advantageous to start with the baton in the right hand, while in others it may be better to begin with the baton in the left hand.

1. APPLY ALL SPRINT START TECHNIQUES AS LEAD MAN IN SPRINT RELAY.

2. HOLD BATON IN FOUR FINGERS WITH THUMB AND KNUCKLES BEHIND STARTING LINE.

3. AT GUN, ENCLOSE
   THUMB AROUND BATON.

4. ANGLE BODY FORWARD
   AND LOW TO GROUND FOR
   FIRST 10 TO 15 YARDS.

5. DRIVE ARMS VIGOROUSLY
   AND RUN WITH KNEES HIGH.

6. ELONGATE STRIDE ONCE
   NATURAL, UPRIGHT
   RUNNING POSITION IS
   ACHIEVED. RUN RELAXED.

Running Through the Passing Zone

In a sprint relay an outgoing runner may stand at a maximum distance of 11 yards preceding the passing zone.

As an outgoing runner, make two marks on the track —a *lean mark* and a *go mark*. As the incoming runner reaches the lean mark, lean forward to prepare for the sprint. When the runner hits the go mark, begin your sprint.

Such distances will vary with each runner, therefore passing partners should practice extensively to determine the correct distances.

The exchange is made at near maximum speed with both runners extending their arms fully.

LEAN   GO

MARK   MARK

11 YARDS   PASSING ZONE — 22 YARDS

1. AS INCOMING RUNNER REACHES LEAN MARK, LEAN FORWARD IN PREPARATION FOR SPRINT. WHEN INCOMING RUNNER REACHES GO MARK, BEGIN SPRINT FOR BATON EXCHANGE WITHIN PASSING ZONE.

2. EXTEND ARMS FULLY FOR EXCHANGE. FORWARD RUNNER LOOKS STRAIGHT AHEAD, NOT BACK.

Exchange Grips

Both the *palm up* and *palm down exchange methods* are used today, but many teams prefer the palm up pass. It seems easier for the incoming man to hand off downward than upward. Also, the outgoing man has the assurance of having his hand underneath the baton which eliminates changing the baton between hands.

A coach should have his relay teams experiment to determine which exchange method is best for them.

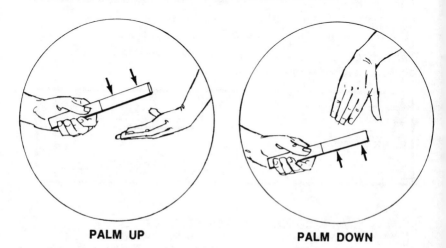

PALM UP   PALM DOWN

Note: For purposes of illustration the exchange pictured is from left hand to right hand which would correspond to the second man passing to the third man, providing the lead-off runner started with the baton in the right hand. If starting with the baton in the left hand, the exchange would correspond to the first and third handoffs.

The Distance Baton Pass

In races over four 220-yard legs, the outgoing runner must start and receive the baton within the 22-yard passing zone area.

The lean mark is eliminated since there is less distance to complete the pass. The distance from the go mark to the point of exchange will vary according to the speed of the incoming runner.

A verbal "go" command is preferred by many teams because it allows the outgoing runner to direct his full effort forward.

Turn the upper portion of body toward the oncoming runner to gauge the exchange in case the runner is greatly fatigued. The pass is made waist high, with palm up and receiving arm fully extended.

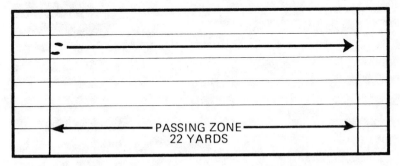

PASSING ZONE
22 YARDS

1. **RUNNER MUST START AND RECEIVE BATON WITHIN 22-YARD PASSING ZONE.**

2. **VERBAL "GO" COMMAND PREFERRED, PERMITTING OUTGOING RUNNER TO DIRECT ATTENTION FORWARD.**

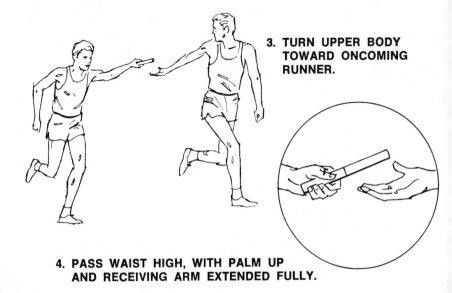

3. **TURN UPPER BODY TOWARD ONCOMING RUNNER.**

4. **PASS WAIST HIGH, WITH PALM UP AND RECEIVING ARM EXTENDED FULLY.**

the long jump

Like the seasoned jumper, the beginning long jumper has one prime objective—that of jumping as far as possible. However, the less experienced jumper may forget that to jump far, one must jump high as well.

The approach run will afford adequate speed to jump far, but the jumper must convert this forward motion to upward motion.

The Approach Run

In practice find a point to start the approach run allowing you to hit the takeoff board without stretching or shortening the stride excessively.

The distance of the run varies among athletes. The distance is usually between 100 and 150 feet. It may take several weeks to establish the correct distance.

A beginning long jumper should remember to run with knees high and keep the body as relaxed as possible to achieve a better takeoff.

Most jumpers use one or more check points for the approach. It is recommended that the beginning jumper use only one check point to gauge the run to the takeoff board and to increase concentration.

1. **PRACTICE APPROACH TO FIND CORRECT DISTANCE TO TAKEOFF BOARD.**

2. **USE CHECK POINT TO GAUGE RUN AND INCREASE CONCENTRATION.**

3. **RUN WITH KNEES HIGH AND BODY RELAXED.**

4. **GENERATE AND MAINTAIN TOP SPEED TO TAKEOFF BOARD.**

Gather, Takeoff, Jump and Landing Techniques

Usually, the last stride to the takeoff board is slightly shorter. The shorter stride allows the body to come forward and over the feet. Lowering the hips provides for more upward thrust.

Keep the head high so as not to look at the board at takeoff.

The heel of the takeoff foot contacts the ground first. The knee is flexed momentarily but straightens as the body rocks forward and over the ball of the foot. This movement is a very explosive action to channel all effort upward.

Providing that you jump off the left foot, drive the right knee and left arm upward at takeoff. This is "opposite arm—opposite leg" action.

On leaving the board, hips and upper body should be well forward of the takeoff foot. Drive the knee of the takeoff leg forward and upward. Rotate the right arm in circle with the left leg. Extend the left foot and then the right.

Once the takeoff leg reaches full forward extension, hold it until the opposite leg comes fully forward in preparation for the landing.

Heels make first contact with the pit from the extended leg position. As heels contact the pit, thrust head and shoulders forward and downward to elevate buttocks. With knees flexed and slightly apart, drop your chin downward between the knees. Fall forward over feet into a support position on hands and knees.

Carry your arms forward and above hip height to aid in the landing, being careful not to drag your fingers in the sand.

1. DURING APPROACH RUN GENERATE SPEED BUT MAINTAIN CONTROL.

2. TAKE SLIGHTLY SHORTER STRIDE TO TAKEOFF BOARD TO BRING BODY OVER FEET. LOWER HIPS FOR MORE UPWARD THRUST.

3. HEEL CONTACTS GROUND FIRST, THEN BODY ROCKS OVER ONTO BALL OF FOOT. DRIVE RIGHT KNEE AND LEFT ARM UPWARD. CHANNEL ALL EFFORT UPWARD.

4. UPON LEAVING TAKEOFF BOARD, HIPS AND UPPER BODY ARE WELL FORWARD OF TAKEOFF FOOT.

5. DRIVE KNEE OF TAKEOFF LEG FORWARD AND UPWARD. ROTATE LEFT ARM IN CIRCLE WITH LEFT LEG.

6. **EXTEND LEFT LEG FULLY AND HOLD TO BRING OPPOSITE LEG FORWARD.**

7. **HEELS CONTACT FIRST FROM EXTENDED LEG POSITION.**

8. **THRUST HEAD AND SHOULDERS FORWARD TO ELEVATE BUTTOCKS. KNEES ARE FLEXED AND SLIGHTLY APART.**

9. **DROP CHIN BETWEEN KNEES AND FALL FORWARD OVER FEET INTO SUPPORT POSITION.**

Note:

During the "jump" phase of the long jump, two distinct styles are used. The *Hitch Hike* or *Step-In-Air* and the *Hang* are styles both widely accepted, and if executed properly, both provide optimum results.

The Step-In-Air style is explained by the foregoing whereas the Hang style is quite self-explanatory in that the jumper projects through the air with legs down and slightly back.

Nearing the completion of the jump, the Hang-style jumper swings his arms and feet forward requiring good abdominal strength.

Step-In-Air Style

Hang Style

the triple jump

To develop the rhythm and coordination necessary to triple jump successfully, it is often best to begin jumping from a standing position first.

The Standing Triple Jump

Stand on the hopping foot and begin by jumping forward to land again on the hopping foot. Then rebound to the opposite foot and jump off that foot into the pit.

The succession of jumps would be: left (start), left, right, both for landing in the pit.

Make a conscious effort to drive the hopping foot down and back just prior to landing before the step phase. Land "flat-footed" for better stability.

When practicing the standing triple jump, keep these important points in mind:

1. **EXECUTE A HOP WHICH CAN BE CONTROLLED UPON LANDING.**

2. **LAND FLAT-FOOTED OVER THE HOPPING FOOT.**

3. **KEEP YOUR CHEST UP.**

4. **DRIVE THE FORWARD LEG UPWARD ON THE STEP, USING YOUR ARMS FOR BALANCE.**

5. **USE ARMS VIGOROUSLY TO LEND POWER TO THE JUMP.**

The Long Step

An excellent method to develop a long step is to mark three lines on the runway approximately two yards apart.

Start from a standing position and hop to the second line. Then step to the third line and jump into the pit. As your ability to reach these lines improves, widen the distance between the marks.

Short Run and Jump

After learning to take an effective step, begin practicing the jump preceded by a short run. Use a five or seven stride approach to the jump. Keep in mind that you must maintain control of the low hop action and keep your chest up while driving the step knee upward.

Failure to keep the chest up results in landing on the hop with the chest over the knee, an impossible position to execute an effective step. A controlled run is essential to maintain balance for proper execution.

Triple Jump Techniques

After you have developed the ability to control fully the short approach jumps, you are ready to jump taking the full approach.

The Approach Run

Essentially, the approach run for the triple jump is the same as for that of the long jump.

However, the takeoff board is moved back approximately 25 feet meaning that a jumper may have to start on the grass, track or in some cases the jumper may have to circle an obstacle such as a pit or rink to get enough distance for the approach run. Consequently, learn to adjust to different runway approaches.

Most importantly, run with control. Obviously, without such control optimum hopping and jumping action is impossible.

1. **MAKE NECESSARY ADJUSTMENTS TO LENGTH OF RUNWAY.**

2. **GENERATE SPEED AND MAINTAIN CONTROL.**

Gather and Takeoff

As contrasted to the long jumper, the triple jumper does not attempt to achieve maximum height during the jump.

The last three strides of the approach run are shortened to move the body into position over the takeoff foot for a more lateral jumping movement. Arms are used to maintain balance.

3. **SHORTEN LAST THREE STRIDES OF APPROACH RUN TO MOVE BODY OVER TAKEOFF FOOT.**

4. **USE ARMS TO MAINTAIN BALANCE.**

Hop Techniques

Take-off on the left foot and drive the right knee forward. Again, the hop is more lateral with less arc.

The lead knee (right knee) circles forward, down and then to the rear while the takeoff foot is brought through with knee high.

With foot forward of the knee land on the ball of the takeoff foot.

5. **TAKE OFF ON LEFT FOOT AND DRIVE RIGHT KNEE FORWARD.**

6. LEAD KNEE CIRCLES
   FORWARD, DOWN AND
   THEN TO REAR.
   BRING TAKEOFF FOOT
   THROUGH WITH KNEE HIGH.
   DO NOT DRAG FOOT
   ON SURFACE.

7. WITH FOOT FORWARD OF
   KNEE, LAND ON BALL OF
   TAKEOFF FOOT.

Step Techniques

Drive the right knee forward and upward forming a 90-degree angle at the knee. Thrust both arms upward vigorously to achieve height.

Bend the trailing leg at the knee to bring the heel of the foot underneath the buttocks. This allows a full, forward carriage of the lead leg through landing on the right foot.

8. DRIVE RIGHT KNEE FORWARD
   AND UPWARD TO FORM
   90-DEGREE ANGLE AT THE
   KNEE. TUCK HEEL OF
   TRAILING FOOT
   UNDERNEATH BUTTOCKS.

9. LAND ON RIGHT FOOT.

Jump Techniques

Spring from the right foot to drive the left leg forward and upward. Extend arms and right leg forward.

Employ Hitch Hike or Hang style techniques as preferred to hold position as long as possible.

10. DRIVE LEFT LEG FORWARD AND UPWARD. EXTEND ARMS AND RIGHT LEG FORWARD.

11. HOLD UPRIGHT POSITION AS LONG AS POSSIBLE.

Landing Techniques

Extend legs forward in circling motion in front of body.

With knees flexed, plant heels first, then thrust the head and shoulders forward and down to a support position on hands and knees.

13. WITH KNEES FLEXED, PLANT HEELS THEN THRUST HEAD AND SHOULDERS FORWARD TO SUPPORT POSITION ON HANDS AND KNEES.

12. EXTEND LEGS FORWARD IN FRONT OF BODY.

the high jump

Although it sounds very elementary, the first thing the beginning high jumper must learn is to jump upward and not forward. Too many young high jumpers become discouraged because they never learn to jump upward.

The Approach

Angle of the approach run varies between 30 and 45 degrees from the face of the crossbar. Most beginning jumpers have better success working closer to a 45-degree angle.

The length of run can vary from seven to eleven strides. Practice from a distance most comfortable for you.

The speed of the run for the most part depends on the strength of the lower body and legs. However, run as fast as possible with control.

1. ANGLE OF RUN VARIES BETWEEN 30 AND 45 DEGREES.

2. LENGTH OF RUN MAY VARY FROM 7 TO 11 STRIDES.
PRACTICE FROM MOST COMFORTABLE AND EFFECTIVE DISTANCE.

3. SPEED IMPORTANT BUT MUST HAVE CONTROL.

Jumping Techniques

The two most basic styles of high jumping are the *Western Roll* and the *Straddle Roll*. It is best for the beginning jumper to learn the western roll first. The straddle roll is much easier to learn once the western roll has been learned correctly.

When learning any style of jumping, first put the crossbar at a height easily attainable.

Western Roll Techniques

Approach the bar from the left side, kick the right leg upward and spring off the left leg. Reverse this action when approaching the jump from the right side.

Prepare for the takeoff approximately three strides from the bar. Flex right knee slightly to initiate kick up motion, but lead with the foot, not with the knee.

Lean back, thrust arms and outside leg upward. With head, shoulders, lead arm and leg above the bar, bring your feet together and clear bar with the left side of the body going over the bar first.

Land on the right foot first then the left.

1. **APPROACH FROM SIDE YOU PREFER AND PREPARE FOR TAKEOFF ABOUT THREE STRIDES FROM THE BAR.**
2. **AT TAKEOFF POINT (APPROXIMATELY ARM'S LENGTH FROM BAR), PLANT INSIDE FOOT WELL IN FRONT OF BODY, LEAN BACK AND DRIVE OUTSIDE ARM AND LEG UPWARD.**
3. **WITH HEAD, SHOULDERS, LEAD ARM AND LEG ABOVE BAR, BRING FEET TOGETHER.**
4. **CLEAR BAR WITH LEFT SIDE OF BODY FIRST.**
5. **LAND ON RIGHT FOOT THEN LEFT.**

Straddle Roll Techniques

The Straddle Roll is a more efficient method of jumping.

Both jumping styles utilize the same, basic approach. Again, speed is important but run with control.

Approach the bar from the left side unless a right-side approach is more natural.

At a distance of three strides from the takeoff point begin to lower the level of the hips. Two steps from the takeoff point, flex the outside knee in preparation for the kick up.

Take one more stride with the outside leg then plant the inside takeoff leg with a vigorous heel stomp. Lay back, drive the arms upward and kick the outside leg up as high as possible.

Head and shoulders go straight up, not toward the crossbar.

At the peak of the jump with head, shoulders, lead arm and leg well above the crossbar, rotate body over and around the crossbar. Stomach faces the crossbar during the entire roll.

Turn the toes of the trailing leg to point skyward. This turning motion keeps the leg high. Do not kick the trailing leg for in kicking the leg, the leg first drops, increasing the possibility of dislodging the crossbar.

Some jumpers prefer to tuck the trailing arm to the chest and tuck the trailing leg heel to buttocks. In this position the trailing arm and leg simply follow the body over and around the bar.

Continue rotation around the bar then lead with head and arm downward to the pit. Land on the right side of your body or on your back. Drop the lead arm and leg first to buffer the fall if the pit is particularly hard.

1. APPROACH BAR FROM LEFT SIDE UNLESS YOU PREFER TO JUMP OFF RIGHT FOOT.

2. RUN WITH SPEED AND CONTROL.

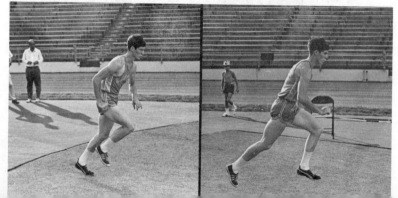

3. THREE STEPS FROM TAKE-OFF, PREPARE FOR TAKEOFF BY LOWERING HIPS.

4. TWO STEPS FROM TAKEOFF, FLEX OUTSIDE KNEE.

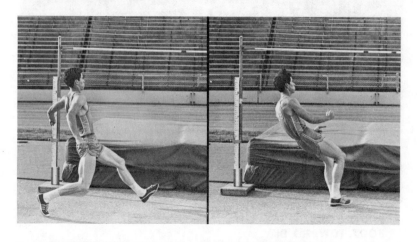

5. AT TAKEOFF POINT, LEAN BACK, PLANT INSIDE HEEL, THRUST ARMS AND OUTSIDE LEG UPWARD.

6. ROTATE ABOVE AND AROUND CROSSBAR AT HEIGHT OF JUMP.

7. POINT TOES OF TRAILING FOOT TOWARD SKY. HEAD AND ARMS START DOWNWARD MOVEMENT TOWARD PIT.

8. LAND ON RIGHT SIDE OR BACK.

The Fosbury Flop

The *Fosbury Flop style* of jumping has gained acceptance and popularity within the past few years.

Dick Fosbury was the first to use this unique style of high jumping most successfully in the 1968 Olympic Games.

It is absolutely necessary to have a very large and soft pit since the jumper lands most often on the upper back and neck area. Injuries may very well occur if the pit is inadequate.

Fosbury Flop Jumping Techniques

One of the advantages of this style is that you may more fully take advantage of the speed generated during the approach run.

Assuming that you approach the bar from the left side, make your approach approximately at a 35-degree angle to the bar.

The Approach

The most unique aspect of this jumping style is that the jumper clears the height with the back facing the bar rather than the stomach or side. Also, the jumper leaps off his outside leg rather than the inside leg.

1. BUILD SPEED DURING APPROACH.

2. MAKE APPROACH AT ABOUT 35-DEGREE ANGLE TO BAR.

The Takeoff and Jump

Do not turn your back to the bar too early but first drive the left knee and right arm upward and jump off the right foot which is the outside foot.

While driving upward, turn the left shoulder slightly away from the bar thus starting the rotational movement of the back toward the bar. As the shoulder reaches a height over the bar, the rotation is such that the back faces the bar. Tip your head back to arch the hips above the crossbar.

As you clear the bar with the hips, raise your knees and forelegs to clear the bar.

Raising the knees and forelegs forces the hips downward. Therefore, it is necessary to wait until the hips are well clear of the bar before raising the knees.

3. DRIVE INSIDE KNEE AND OUTSIDE ARM UPWARD, AND JUMP OFF OUTSIDE FOOT.

4. TURN INSIDE SHOULDER
   AWAY FROM BAR TO START
   ROTATIONAL MOVEMENT
   OF BACK TO BAR.
   BACK FACES BAR AS
   SHOULDER ACHIEVES
   HEIGHT ABOVE BAR.

5. ARCH BACK AND HIPS
   ABOVE CROSSBAR.

6. WITH HIPS CLEAR OF BAR, RAISE KNEES THEN
   FORELEGS ABOVE AND OVER BAR.

7. LAND ON UPPER
   PORTION OF BACK.

the pole vault

The pole vault is one of the most spectacular and exciting events in all of sports. As much as any sports event, the pole vault demands strength, coordination and conditioning.

The Grip

Spread hands from 12 to 24 inches with the top hand a minimum of six inches below a point on the pole equal to the height of the attempted vault.

1. SPREAD HANDS 12 TO 24 INCHES APART. BACKS OF BOTH HANDS FACE UPWARD.

2. TOP HAND IS A MINIMUM OF SIX INCHES BELOW POINT ON POLE EQUAL TO HEIGHT OF ATTEMPTED VAULT.

The Pole Carry

Carry the "plug end" of the pole not higher than 12 inches above eye level nor lower than a plane parallel with the runway.

Hold the pole slightly across the body, making adjustments for comfort.

1. CARRY POLE NOT HIGHER THAN 12 INCHES ABOVE EYE LEVEL NOR LOWER THAN PLANE PARALLEL WITH RUNWAY.

2. HOLD POLE SLIGHTLY ACROSS BODY.

The Approach

Begin by standing on the approach mark. Running to this mark may cause you to vary your takeoff point as much as 12 inches.

To achieve maximum running speed, experiment to find the correct length of run for you. This distance may vary from time to time.

1. STAND ON APPROACH.

2. BEGIN RUN FROM APPROACH MARK.

Vaulting Techniques

At a distance of about three strides from the pole box, begin to raise the pole overhead.

With the pole directly above the head, slide the pole into the box. Keep the pole away from the body and in front.

A beginning vaulter should slide the bottom hand within two or three inches of the top hand to provide additional leverage for the swing forward and upward. **As vaulting skill advances, discontinue bringing hands together.** When the pole strikes the back of the box, drive the right knee upward and spring off the left foot. Swing upward to begin curling action.

Bring knees to the chest and point heels upward. To facilitate good leg action, throw the head back.

Extend the arms fully and pull with maximum strength and power to project both feet over the bar.

Continue pull to elevate hips above and over the crossbar. As the pole begins to return to an upright position, cross the right leg over the left to roll the hips and trunk. The entire body faces the bar.

Vigorously, push off from the pole with feet pointed toward the back of the pit. Throw arms overhead to clear the bar. Do not push chest forward to hit the crossbar.

3. **THREE STEPS FROM TAKEOFF, SHIFT POLE FORWARD AND BEGIN CURLING ACTION.**

4. **TWO STEPS FROM TAKEOFF, POLE AT EAR HEIGHT OR SLIGHTLY ABOVE.**

5. **ONE STEP FROM TAKEOFF, PLANT POLE WITH BOTH HANDS DIRECTLY OVERHEAD. TOP ARM IS FULLY EXTENDED.**

6. AT TAKEOFF POINT, DRIVE LEAD LEG FORWARD FORMING 90-DEGREE ANGLE AT KNEE. SPRING OFF TRAILING LEG.

7. BRING LEGS TOWARD CHEST AND POINT HEELS UPWARD. PULL WITH MAXIMUM STRENGTH. BACK IS PARALLEL WITH RUNWAY.

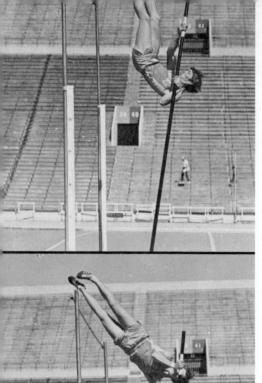

8. **CONTINUE PULLING MOTION.**

9. **ELEVATE LEGS AND HIPS ABOVE CROSSBAR. KEEP LOWER ARM ELBOW TUCKED INSIDE OF POLE.**

10. **AS HIPS CLEAR CROSS-BAR, CROSS RIGHT LEG OVER LEFT LEG (RIGHT-HANDED VAULTER). HIPS AND TRUNK TWIST TO FACE BAR.**

11. RELEASE FROM POLE, THROWING ARMS OVERHEAD SO AS NOT TO HIT BAR.

12. DO NOT THROW ARMS BACK SO FAR AS TO PROJECT CHEST FORWARD TO STRIKE BAR.

13. LAND ON BACK.

How to Correct Common Vaulting Faults

1. Planting the pole with the body ending up on the left side of the pole. The pole should be directly above the head. Practice walking through the proper method of planting the pole at least 10 times a day. All good vaulters do this.

2. Planting the pole too close to body. The arms are not in front, therefore the body cannot "swing." During the plant, the left arm must be raised and held in front of the body.

3. Problem of rocking back to bring knees up. If this is the situation you probably are not holding your head back which helps to bring the feet up more quickly.

4. Not strong enough to really pull. This problem can be corrected by weight lifting and exercises.

the shot put

The Celts originated shot putting which gained popularity in Scotland and Ireland where it first was known as "putting the stone."

Colleges and universities use a 16-pound shot while high schools use a 12-pound shot and junior high schools, an eight-pound ball.

The Grip

Rest the shot at the base of the index and two middle fingers. The thumb and little finger provide support. The shot should lie slightly toward the thumb and index finger. When control permits, move the little finger more behind the shot than to the side.

1. **REST SHOT AT BASE OF INDEX AND TWO MIDDLE FINGERS. DO NOT SPREAD FINGERS EXCESSIVELY.**

2. **THUMB AND LITTLE FINGER PROVIDE SUPPORT.**

Starting Position

Place the shot in the hollow area adjacent to the rear process of the jaw. The elbow of the putting arm supports the weight of the shot.

A right-handed putter places the right foot to the back of the circle, flat upon the surface with toes close to the rim. Usually with the toes, the opposite foot makes light contact with the surface, some 16 to 20 inches from the right foot.

With head up, focus your eyes on some object 12 to 18 feet in a direct line opposite to the direction of the throw.

1. **HOLD SHOT AGAINST HOLLOW PROCESS ADJACENT TO JAW.**

2. **POINT ELBOW AWAY FROM BODY.**

3. **RIGHT FOOT IS FLAT UPON SURFACE WITH TOES CLOSE TO RIM.**

   OPPOSITE FOOT TOUCHES SURFACE LIGHTLY 16 TO 20 INCHES BEHIND.

4. **HEAD UP WITH EYES FOCUSED ON POINT IN LINE DIRECTLY OPPOSITE TO DIRECTION OF THROW.**

Putting Techniques

From the starting position, drop the center of gravity by flexing the right knee. Bring the left knee close to the planted leg as the head and upper body dip down.

Shift weight toward the center of the circle, extending the left leg toward the toe board. Drive powerfully off the right leg to hop to the center of the circle. Keep your head and eyes up.

Left and right feet should be planted almost simultaneously. Toes of the left foot touch the toe board while the heel forms a 10-degree angle with the board.

Continue the motion forward and do not dip the shot downward. Lead with the free arm and hip in a forward, lifting motion. Turn the hips and trunk, leaning backward slightly to keep shot in a straight line.

Shot remains against the neck as the elbow moves into a "high" position.

Keep the elbow high with foot in contact with the ground as long as possible. The thumb is well in toward the center of the body.

Keep the shot moving in an upward, forward line to release the shot from the fingers with a distinct wrist snap.

As the shot leaves the fingers, bring the rear foot forward to the toe board while shifting the left leg to the center of the circle. Lower hips to drop center of gravity over front foot.

Putting arm follows in a complete motion across the body. Keep the head in line with the throw.

1. FROM STARTING POSITION, DROP CENTER OF GRAVITY BY FLEXING RIGHT KNEE.

2. BRING LEFT KNEE CLOSE TO PLANTED LEG AS HEAD AND UPPER BODY DIP DOWN.

3. WITH A HOPPING MOTION SHIFT WEIGHT TOWARD CENTER OF CIRCLE.

4. EXTEND LEFT LEG TOWARD TOE BOARD.

5. LEFT AND RIGHT FEET CONTACT SURFACE NEARLY SIMULTANEOUSLY.

6. LEAD WITH FREE ARM AND LEFT SIDE OF BODY IMPARTING A FORWARD, LIFTING MOTION.

7. KEEP ELBOW HIGH WITH BOTH FEET IN CONTACT WITH SURFACE AS LONG AS POSSIBLE. DRIVE BODY UPWARD OFF THE BENT RIGHT LEG UTILIZING POWER OF TRUNK AND LEG MUSCLES.

9. AS SHOT LEAVES FINGERS, BRING REAR LEG FORWARD TO TOE BOARD WHILE SHIFTING FRONT LEG BACKWARD.

8. KEEP SHOT MOVING IN AN UPWARD, FORWARD LINE. ACCELERATE WITH CONTINUOUS MOTION. RELEASE SHOT FROM FINGERS WITH DISTINCT SNAP OF WRIST.

10. DROP CENTER OF GRAVITY OVER FRONT LEG. PUTTING ARM FOLLOWS THROUGH IN COMPLETE MOTION ACROSS BODY. HEAD REMAINS IN LINE WITH THROW.

The Side-Style Shot-Put Method

Many beginning shot putters have better success learning the *Side-style method* first when proceeding to the method presented previously which is sometimes referred to as the *O'Brien Form* named after Perry O'Brien, longtime, great shot putter.

The Practice Throw

Before practicing the complete motion, begin by making a series of standing throws to become accustomed to the shot itself.

Stand with legs spread slightly more than a shoulder's-width apart and with the left shoulder in line to the direction of the throw.

Practice driving the body up when making these throws. Also, practice hopping across the circle without the shot to get the feel of the complete putting motion.

Side-Style Techniques

A right-handed thrower should stand with body at a 90-degree angle to the direction of the throw.

Cradle the shot in the hollow portion behind the jaw. Flex the knee of the right leg slightly and crouch over this leg to support weight. Shot is positioned directly over the right foot.

The right leg remains bent to start the glide and to land in the middle of the circle. The left foot leads the action.

From the bent leg position, start the throw by driving upward with the legs and body, rotating hips, trunk and shoulders in the direction of the throw.

Push the shot forward with a powerful snap of the wrist and arm. Action of the arm is rapid with great strength. Motion is continuous from start to finish.

Swing arm across the chest to complete the follow through and reverse the position of the feet so that the right foot comes forward to support the body.

Points to Remember Are:

1. LEG POWER IS MOST IMPORTANT.
   MAKE GOOD USE OF THE TREMENDOUS
   STRENGTH AND LIFT IMPARTED
   BY THE LEGS.

2. PRACTICE TO COORDINATE BODY
   STRENGTH AND MOMENTUM WITH THE
   THROWING ACTION.

3. PRACTICE THE GLIDE ACROSS THE
   CIRCLE, FIRST WITHOUT THE SHOT
   THEN WITH.

4. EXERCISE AND RUN TO BUILD
   STRENGTH AND STAMINA.

the discus throw

Discus throwing has evolved considerably since the days of the famous, ancient Greek athletes.

Today, the discus is constructed of hard rubber or of wood with a metal rim.

The Grip

Hold the discus in the left hand and slide the palm of the right hand across the face to a position where the first joints of the four fingers are over the edge. The fingers are spread with the thumb pressing upon the discus.

1. PALM OF THROWING HAND FLAT UPON FACE OF DISCUS.

2. FINGERS SPREAD, FIRST JOINT OF FINGERS OVER EDGE WITH THUMB PRESSING AGAINST DISCUS.

The Standing Throw

To get the feel of the throwing motion and release, practice throwing from a standing position.

Stand in the direction of the throw with legs slightly bent and feet a shoulder's-width apart. Right foot is near the center of the circle and left foot near the edge of the circle in the direction of the throw.

Take a number of practice swings extending the throwing arm as far back as possible. On the final swing, bend at the knees and pull the left arm across the chest.

Drive up with the right leg and swing the right arm around slightly below shoulder level to release the discus off the index finger.

Release off the index finger is vital. If this release is difficult, merely roll the discus along the ground to practice releasing the discus off the index finger until this release becomes more natural.

Learn control at this level, not how hard you can throw.

1. **STAND IN DIRECTION OF THROW WITH LEGS SLIGHTLY BENT AND FEET A SHOULDER'S-WIDTH APART.**

2. **TAKE TWO OR THREE PRACTICE SWINGS, EXTENDING THE THROWING ARM AS FAR BACK AS POSSIBLE. ON FINAL SWING, BEND KNEES AND BRING NON-THROWING ARM ACROSS CHEST.**

3. **DRIVE UP WITH THE RIGHT LEG AND SWING RIGHT ARM AROUND SLIGHTLY BELOW SHOULDER LEVEL TO RELEASE DISCUS OFF INDEX FINGER.**

Discus Throw Techniques

After developing the ability to control the throw from a standing position, begin to throw utilizing the full turn.

Stand to the rear of the circle so that the left shoulder faces the direction of the throw when turned in a counterclockwise position.

Feet are a shoulder's-width apart with legs slightly bent. Point toes of the left foot toward the outside of the circle. Keep weight over the right leg and take a few swings to relax the upper body.

Lead with the left knee into the circle. Pivot on the ball of the left foot while shifting your weight over the left foot. Throwing arm trails the entire turning movement. Look over the left shoulder toward the direction of the throw and drive the right foot to the center of the circle.

With a pronounced forward shoulder lean, bring the right leg around the left leg, leading with the knee. Keep the arm straight and the disc close to the hips.

Both feet come off the ground momentarily, landing very quickly with the right then the left. The right foot lands approximately in the middle of the circle facing about the same direction as when starting.

With weight over the right leg, drive off the right leg leading with the hip and left arm. Keep the shoulders, right arm and discus back as long as possible.

1. STAND TO REAR OF RING SO THAT LEFT SHOULDER POINTS IN DIRECTION OF THROW WHEN TURNED IN COUNTERCLOCKWISE DIRECTION.

**2. FEET ARE SHOULDER'S-WIDTH APART WITH LEGS SLIGHTLY BENT AND WEIGHT OVER RIGHT LEG.
TAKE SEVERAL SWINGS TO RELAX AND PREPARE.**

Pull discus from far behind the body with trunk and shoulders leading the movement. Keep the discus out and away from the body to make the release at shoulder height in front of the chest.

Snap shoulders and hips at the release while pressing the thumb downward.

As the discus leaves the throwing hand and fingers, rotate the rear foot forward and release the opposite foot to swing to the rear.

Lower your hips, dropping the center of gravity over the front foot to keep within the ring. The throwing arm follows in a complete motion across the body.

3. EXTEND ARM BACK AS FAR AS POSSIBLE.

4. LEAD WITH LEFT KNEE, PIVOT ON BALL OF LEFT FOOT AND SHIFT WEIGHT OVER LEFT FOOT.

THROWING ARM TRAILS TURNING MOVEMENT.

5. BRING RIGHT LEG AROUND LEFT, LEADING WITH THE KNEE.

KEEP ARMS STRAIGHT AND DISC CLOSE TO HIPS.

6. **BOTH FEET COME OFF GROUND MOMENTARILY, LANDING FIRST THE RIGHT FOOT THEN THE LEFT.**

   RIGHT FOOT LANDS IN CENTER OF CIRCLE FACING STARTING DIRECTION.

7. **WITH WEIGHT OVER RIGHT LEG, DRIVE OFF RIGHT LEG LEADING WITH LEFT HIP AND ARM. KEEP DISCUS BACK AS LONG AS POSSIBLE.**

8. **PULL DISCUS FROM FAR IN BACK OF BODY WITH TRUNK AND SHOULDERS LEADING MOVEMENT.**

9. KEEP DISCUS OUT AND
   AWAY FROM BODY TO
   RELEASE AT SHOULDER
   HEIGHT IN FRONT OF
   CHEST.

10. SNAP SHOULDERS AND
    HIPS AT RELEASE WHILE
    PRESSING THUMB DOWN.

11. UPON RELEASE, ROTATE REAR FOOT FORWARD AND
    RELEASE OPPOSITE FOOT TO SWING TO REAR.
    LOWER HIPS, DROPPING CENTER OF GRAVITY OVER THE
    FRONT FOOT TO KEEP WITHIN RING.

Overcoming Basic Mistakes

Many beginning throwers make the mistakes listed below. Be careful not to make the errors.

1. Failure to bend legs so as not assume "a sitting position" when starting the turn.

2. Failure to keep the thumb pressing down on the discus and the discus points upon release.

3. Spinning too fast to lose control on the turn. Result is a throw without power.

4. Allowing the discus to "creep" forward during the spin with the result that in the final throwing position the discus is too far forward to make a full effort.

5. Keeping the throwing arm too close to the body. This will cause the thrower to throw the discus in a scooping manner. The flight of the discus will be too high.

6. Not driving the body forward and upward on delivery. Failure to keep the shoulders moving forward therefore using only the arm to throw the discus causes loss of power.

7. Falling off balance by looking down or up. The continued horizontal focus of the eyes implies that the line of the shoulders also will be held close to a horizontal position.

the javelin

Throwing the javelin evolved from the primitive practice of spearing fish and animals for food. The Swedes and the Finns were the first to introduce this event to modern athletic programs.

A javelin is a long spear with a metal tip weighing not less than 1¾ pounds.

The Grip

The javelin is held to lie diagonally across the palm of the hand. The palm actually grips the javelin with the index finger or index and second fingers wrapped around the shaft near the rear portion of the cord.

Do not grip the shaft too tightly, only enough to insure control.

1. **HOLD JAVELIN TO LIE DIAGONALLY ACROSS PALM OF HAND.**

2. **PALM GRIPS JAVELIN WITH INDEX OR INDEX AND SECOND FINGERS WRAPPED AROUND SHAFT TOUCHING CORD.**

3. **DO NOT GRIP TOO TIGHTLY.**

4. **USE GRIP WHICH SUITS YOU BEST.**

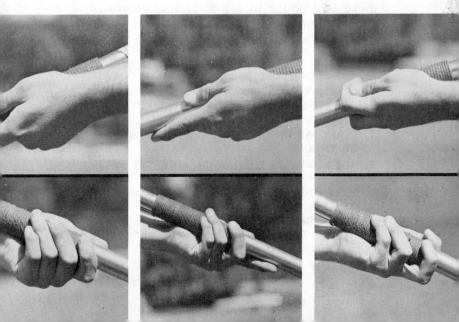

Learning to Throw

Before throwing from a running approach, the beginning thrower should practice throwing from a standing position. Start by taking several short throws. Stand at a right angle to the direction in which you plan to throw. Hold the javelin so the tip is at eye level with the right arm held straight back. The legs are spread approximately one yard apart and are on the same horizontal line.

Shift your weight back over the rear leg. The legs and the trunk must initiate the throw with the arm following. In the throwing action the elbow precedes the forearm. Many beginners tend to throw the javelin with a very stiff arm action; this is a mistake and should be corrected immediately.

Although the throwing arm is held stiffly just prior to the throw, in the actual throw the arm bends and the elbow comes just over the ear, followed by the hand. The motion is very similar to throwing a small ball. During the throw, the left leg is directly in line with the right leg and is bent only slightly. The body straightens as it comes over the left leg giving a slightly upward force to the body.

The wrist follows in the direction of the flight of the javelin. The coach should be careful in explaining these techniques to his throwers. Otherwise, it might be confusing so as to cause them to mis-time their throws.

One point to remember: do not bring the tip of the javelin above head level prior to the throw. The point of the javelin should be pointed directly in line with the direction of the throw.

1. **STAND AT RIGHT ANGLES TO DIRECTIONS OF THROW.**
2. **HOLD JAVELIN WITH ARM STRAIGHT BACK AND TIP AT EYE LEVEL.**
3. **LEGS AND TRUNK INITIATE THROW FOLLOWED BY ARM.**
4. **KEEP ARM IN RIGID POSITION PRIOR TO THROW. ARM BENDS, ELBOW COMES OVER EAR FOLLOWED BY HAND.**
5. **FOLLOW THROUGH IN DIRECTION OF THROW.**

Javelin Throwing Techniques

The Approach and Carry Position

The best approach is that which allows you to maintain maximum momentum and places you in the most effective throwing position.

Stand on a premeasured check point approximately 80 to 125 feet from the toe board. Hold the javelin at ear level over the shoulder and parallel with the ground.

Length of the run will vary with different athletes depending on how long it takes to get to a controlled, top speed before reaching the delivery point. Experiment to find the optimum distance for you.

1. **STAND ON PREMEASURED CHECK POINT ABOUT 80 TO 125 FEET FROM TOE BOARD.**

2. **HOLD JAVELIN AT EAR LEVEL OR SLIGHTLY HIGHER, OVER SHOULDER AND PARALLEL WITH GROUND.**

Crossover Steps

The crossover steps are those delivery steps taken just prior to the point of release.

At a second, premeasured check mark, usually about 20 to 25 feet from the toe board, the first of a series of crossover steps is taken.

The actual crossover means that the right-handed thrower crosses the right foot over the left or the left-handed thrower crosses the left foot over the right while facing at a right angle to the direction of the throw.

On the first crossover step, the toes of the crossover foot point in an approximately 45-degree angle to the direction of the throw. On the second cross-over step the body should turn to a full, 90-degree angle to the throw. At this point the thrower is running sideways, crossing the back leg over the forward leg.

On the final crossover step, the body is leaning back and over the bent rear leg. Also at this point, the throwing arm is extended back fully in position for the throw.

1. AT CHECK MARK, INITIATE CROSSOVER STEPS TO POSITION BODY FOR THROW. REAR FOOT CROSSES OVER FORWARD FOOT.

2. BODY AT 90-DEGREE ANGLE TO DIRECTION OF THROW DURING SIDEWAYS APPROACH.

3. WITH THE FINAL CROSSOVER STEP, BODY IS LEANING OVER REAR LEG AND THROWING ARM IS EXTENDED BACK FULLY.

Throw Techniques

Utilize good carry and crossover step technique to put you in the most advantageous position to begin throwing motion.

The chest is turned toward the javelin to facilitate the full arm extension. With the final crossover step the leg is positioned in such a way that the toe points inward toward the runway. Weight is over the rear leg.

Lean back as far as possible while maintaining forward momentum. As the front foot strides forward, the rear foot initiates throwing motion. Hips then rotate followed by the trunk, shoulders and finally the throwing arm. The arm pulls straight over the shoulder with the elbow leading the hand.

Release the javelin while rotating up and over the extended forward leg. Note that head and chin drop slightly away from the javelin, however all action is upward and forward to the direction of flight.

To complete the throw and follow through, the rear leg continues forward and is planted at a 90-degree angle to the toe board.

It is important to flex the knee of the back leg and drop the level of the hips to slow the momentum and prevent crossing the toe board.

1. EXECUTE GOOD CARRY AND CROSSOVER STEP TECHNIQUES.

2. TURN CHEST TOWARD JAVELIN.

3. LEAN BACK ON REAR LEG, BUT MAINTAIN FORWARD MOMENTUM.

4. INITIATE THROWING
   MOTION WITH REAR FOOT.

   HIPS ROTATE FOLLOWED
   BY TRUNK, SHOULDERS
   AND THROWING ARM.

   ARM PULLS STRAIGHT
   OVER SHOULDER WITH
   ELBOW LEADING HAND.

5. RELEASE JAVELIN, ROTATING UP AND
   OVER EXTENDED FORWARD LEG.

6. COMPLETE THROW AND FOLLOW THROUGH.
   CONTINUE REAR LEG FORWARD.

   FLEX KNEE OF REAR LEG AND DROP
   LEVEL OF HIPS TO SLOW MOMENTUM.

dimensions

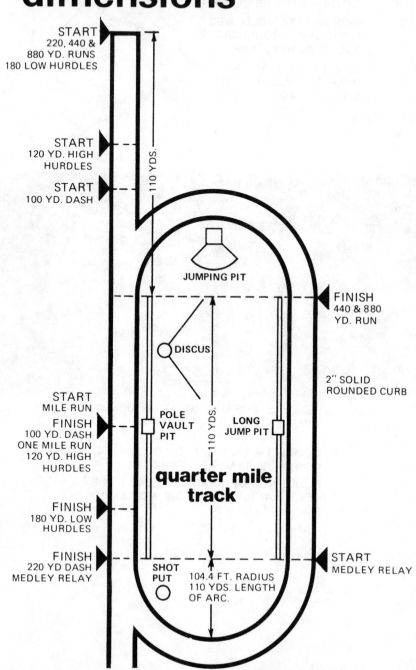

START
220, 440 &
880 YD. RUNS
180 LOW HURDLES

START
120 YD. HIGH
HURDLES

START
100 YD. DASH

110 YDS.

JUMPING PIT

FINISH
440 & 880
YD. RUN

DISCUS

2" SOLID
ROUNDED CURB

START
MILE RUN

FINISH
100 YD. DASH
ONE MILE RUN
120 YD. HIGH
HURDLES

POLE
VAULT
PIT

LONG
JUMP PIT

110 YDS.

quarter mile
track

FINISH
180 YD. LOW
HURDLES

FINISH
220 YD DASH
MEDLEY RELAY

SHOT
PUT

104.4 FT. RADIUS
110 YDS. LENGTH
OF ARC.

START
MEDLEY RELAY

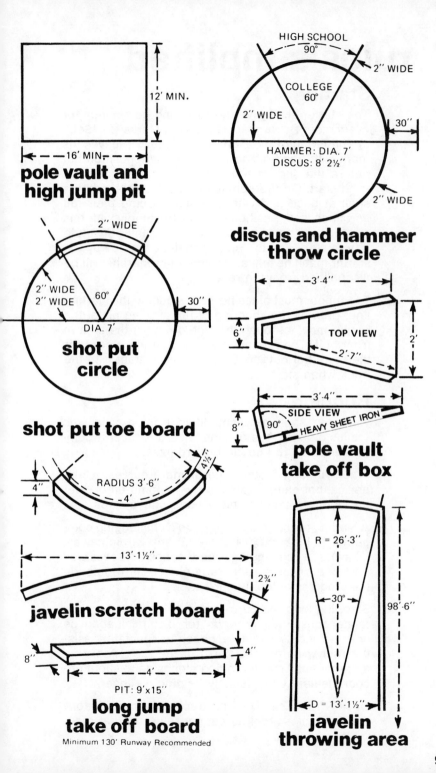

pole vault and high jump pit

12' MIN.
16' MIN.

discus and hammer throw circle

HIGH SCHOOL 90°
COLLEGE 60°
2" WIDE
2" WIDE
2" WIDE
30"
HAMMER: DIA. 7'
DISCUS: 8' 2½''

shot put circle

2" WIDE
2" WIDE
2" WIDE
60°
30"
DIA. 7'

shot put toe board

3'-4''
6''
TOP VIEW
2'-7''
2'

pole vault take off box

3'-4''
8''
90°
SIDE VIEW
HEAVY SHEET IRON

RADIUS 3'-6''
4''
4½''
4'

javelin scratch board

13'-1½''.
2¾''

long jump take off board

8''
4''
4'
PIT: 9'x15''
Minimum 130' Runway Recommended

javelin throwing area

R = 26'-3''
30°
98'-6''
D = 13'-1½''

93

rules simplified

Starting

The starter shall give the following commands for every race: 1) "Runners Go to Your Marks" 2) "Set," 3) The Firing of the Gun. If a competitor leaves his mark with hand or foot after the "set" position but before the shot is fired, it shall be considered a false start. On the command "set" all competitors shall at once and without delay assume their full and final "set" position. Failure to comply with this command after a reasonable time shall constitute a false start, and the runner shall be warned by the starter that if he makes another false start he will be disqualified from the race.

The runner must place his hands behind the starting line; prior to the shooting of the starting pistol the runner may not touch this line or any of the area in front of it. The runners may use starting blocks for their feet but both feet must be in contact with the track when starting.

Running

A runner shall be disqualified from a race who jostles, cuts across or otherwise obstructs a competitor so as to impede his progress.

When running around one or more curves, a runner cannot gain advantage by stepping on or over his lane line, three or more consecutive steps.

A leading runner cannot impede a challenging competitor to his right or left on the final straightaway. Likewise, a challenging runner cannot force his way past one or more runners ahead so as to impede the progress of the runner(s).

Stepping onto the curb to shorten the running distance constitutes grounds for disqualification as does having a teammate, coach or spectator assist the runner before the finish of the race. Assisting a runner shall mean running alongside to shout encouragement or physically helping a runner.

Once a runner leaves the track voluntarily before the finish of a race, he cannot return to that race.

Hurdles

There are three official hurdle races.

	HEIGHT		DISTANCE START TO FIRST HURDLE	DISTANCE BETWEEN HURDLES	DISTANCE LAST HURDLE TO FINISH	TOTAL DISTANCE	
	H.S.	COLL.				H.S.	COLL.
HIGH HURDLES	39″	42″	15 Yards	10 Yards	15 Yards	120 Yards	120 Yards
LOW HURDLES	30″	—	20 Yards	20 Yards	20 Yards	180 Yards	—
400 INTERMEDIATE HURDLES	36″	36″	49.213 Yards	38.272 Yards	46.5 Yards	440 Yards	440 Yards

A hurdler may knock down any number of hurdles without being disqualified from the race. However, a competitor who runs around or carries his leg or foot alongside any hurdle shall be disqualified.

For the rules which govern the starting of a hurdle race refer to the foregoing **rules simplified** section entitled "Starting."

Relay Race

The same rules and penalties apply to relay race competition as for other running events.

If any member of a relay team is disqualified, the team is disqualified.

A runner may carry the baton in either hand, but cannot transport the baton otherwise. The baton must be passed within the 22-yard passing zone.

After passing the baton, a runner cannot veer into another lane so as to impede the progress of a competitor.

For complete track and field rules information, consult the following sources:

College Athletics Publishing Service (NCAA)
347 East Thomas Road
Phoenix, Arizona 85012

National Federation of State High Schools Assn.
400 Leslie Street
Elgin, Illinois 60120

American Athletic Union (AAU)
AAU House
231 West 58th Street
New York, New York 10019

The Long Jump

In a meet involving two teams, each individual is allowed four jumps. The best of the four jumps is the competitor's record for that meet. In a meet involving more than two teams each competitor is allowed three jumps in the finals. The number of qualifiers for the finals corresponds to the number of awards to be given plus one. Example: If five medals are to be awarded then six competitors will qualify for the finals. If a jumper has a better jump in the preliminaries than in the finals, the preliminary jump shall count as his record for the meet.

Any part of the foot touching the ground on the pit side of the take off board during the take off the jump is considered a foul, and as such will not be measured but will count as an attempt. Also, if the jumper runs past the take off board, a foul is recorded.

The measurement of the jumps shall be made at right angles from the take off board, or the take off board extended to the nearest break in the ground (pit) made by the individual.

The Triple Jump

The competitor shall first land upon the same foot on which he started the take off. The opposite foot shall be used for the second landing, and both feet shall be used for the third landing. In all other respects the rules for the long jump shall apply.

The High Jump

The high jumper is allowed three attempts at each height. If he misses one height with three consecutive jumps, he is eliminated from the competition, whereas the best height which he successfully cleared is listed as his record for that day. If the jumper runs at the bar, decides not to jump but runs under the bar, an attempt is registered. If any part of his body projects under or over the bar, an attempt is counted.

A jumper must jump off one foot.

The Pole Vault

The rules which govern the pole vault are the same as those of the high jump with the following considerations:

1. For an attempt to be considered a vault, the vaulter must either leave the ground or touch with his pole or body any of the area on the pit side of the crossbar.

2. The pole may have a binding of not more than two layers of adhesive tape.

The pole vault box has the following dimensions: Width (edge closest to runway) 24 inches and (edge furthermost away) six inches. Sides are 40 inches long. The stopboard, which sits at a 90-degree angle to the bottom of the box, is six inches wide flaring to 14 inches with a depth of eight inches. The box should be constructed in such a manner that the sides slope outward from the end nearest the pit.

The Shot Put

The university and open division shot putters must throw a ball which weighs 16 pounds. Shot putters who are members of secondary school teams normally use a shot which weighs 12 pounds. For those competitors who are very young (grade school age) a six pound shot is recommended.

The shot putter is allowed to throw the shot from within a circle with a diameter of seven feet. At no time during the throw may he step either on the boundary of the circle or step out of the circle. After he has made his throw he must walk out of the back half of the circle. In a meet which only involves two teams, each competitor is allowed four throws. In a meet with many teams entered, each competitor is allowed three throws in the preliminaries, and if qualifying for the finals, three throws in the finals. The number of qualifiers is determined by adding one place to the number of places which will count as scores.

The Discus

The discus thrower must throw within a circle with a diameter eight feet 2½ inches. In making his throw the discus thrower must not touch the edge of the circle or the ground outside it with any part of his body. He must not leave the circle until the discus has landed and he must leave from a standing position from the rear half of the circle.

The measurement must be made from the nearest edge of the mark first made in the ground by the discus to the inner edge of the circle along a line drawn from the mark to the center of the circle. The discus must land within a sector which forms a 60-degree angle extended from the center of the circle.

The discus thrown by competitors in the university or open division weighs four pounds 6½ ounces and has a diameter of 8¾ inches. The high school discus weighs three pounds nine ounces and has a diameter of 8¼ inches.

The Javelin

The weight of a javelin is one pound 12¼ ounces. A javelin may measure in length from eight feet 6⅜ inches to eight feet 10¼ inches.

The javelin shall consist of three parts: a metal head, a shaft and a cord grip. The shaft may be constructed of either wood or metal. The shaft at its thickest point may not measure less than one inch nor more than 1-9/50 inches. The cord grip may not measure less than six inches nor more than 6-5/16 inches.

The javelin must be held by the grip, with one hand only, and so that the little finger is nearest to the point. The thrower's last contact with the javelin shall be with the grip.

At no time after preparing to throw until the javelin has been thrown in the air may the competitor turn completely around so that his back is towards the throwing area. The javelin shall be thrown over the shoulder or upper part of the throwing arm and may not be thrown with an underhand motion.

No throw shall be valid or counted in which the tip of the point of the javelin does not strike the ground before any other part of the shaft.

exercise and training

Sprint Exercises

A sprinter should practice his start over a distance of 15 to 30 yards every day. As a sprinter practice concentrating on your starts. Calisthenics should include toe touches, sit ups, push ups, leg lifts, toe raises, half squats and squeezing a rubber ball. Run with a high knee lift. Practice standing in place and moving your arms in the correct starting movements.

Hurdles Exercises

Sit ups every day help to strengthen the abdominal muscles.

Practice sitting on the ground in a hurdling position. With practice you should be able to touch your head to your forward knee. Your back leg should be at a 90-degree angle with the forward leg.

Also, practice kicking the lead leg as though there were a hurdle in front of you.

Run with long bouncy strides. Lift your knees high when you run.

The start should be practiced every day. The hurdler who arrives at the first hurdle first has the advantage of putting pressure on his fellow competitors to catch up.

Practice "side hurdling." Run alongside the hurdle and simply pull only the trail leg over the hurdle.

Go through the regular workout every day. For a hurdler to run a good race he must be in excellent condition.

Training for the 880-Yard Run and Mile Run

Ideally, an athlete should train six full months before his first race. However, custom in most areas does not afford such extensive preliminary conditioning for runner. Four weeks or less are usually available for preliminary conditioning prior to the first competition in the spring.

The following is a four week "crash training" schedule suggested by former Olympian Fred Wilt for young men training for the mile and half-mile races.

All workouts can be completed within 90 minutes. If the track is wet and soggy, merely mark off distances accurately on a road and run the recommended repetitions with the wind, returning against the wind for recovery. Times are quoted hereafter for the purpose of illustration. Generally speaking, 110-yard repetitions need not be timed.

FIRST WEEK

SATURDAY 10 x 110 yards in 20 seconds each. Walk 110 yards after each.

SUNDAY 12 x 110 yards in 20 seconds each. Walk 110 yards after each.

MONDAY 14 x 110 yards in 20 seconds each. Walk 110 yards after each.

TUESDAY 16 x 110 yards in 20 seconds each. Walk 110 yards after each.

WEDNESDAY 20 x 110 yards in 20 seconds each. Walk 110 yards after each.

THURSDAY Warm up. Run 2 miles in 15 minutes or less. Walk 10 minutes. 5 x 150 yards, acceleration runs. An acceleration run means jog 50 yards, stride 50 yards and sprint 50 yards. Then walk 50 yards before starting the next.

FRIDAY Rest or makeup day.

SECOND WEEK

SATURDAY 20 x 110 yards in 20 seconds. Jog and walk alternately for 110 yards after each.

SUNDAY 10 x 440 yards in 80 seconds. Walk three minutes after each.

MONDAY 10 x 220 yards in 35 seconds. Walk 220 yards in three minutes or less after each.

TUESDAY 10 x 440 yards in 80 seconds. Walk two minutes after each.

WEDNESDAY	25 x 110 yards in 20 seconds. Walk and jog after each.
THURSDAY	Two miles in 15 minutes or less. Walk 10 minutes. 10 x 15 yards acceleration runs.
FRIDAY	Rest or makeup day.

THIRD WEEK

SATURDAY	30 x 110 yards in 18-20 seconds. Walk or jog 110 yards after each.
SUNDAY	10 x 440 yards in 75 seconds. Walk two minutes after each.
MONDAY	10 x 220 yards in 32-34 seconds. Walk and jog 220 yards in three minutes or less after each.
TUESDAY	6-10 x 660 yards in two minutes each (80 seconds per 440 yards pace.) Walk 220 yards in three minutes after each.
WEDNESDAY	30 x 110 yards in 16-18 seconds. Walk 110 yards after each.
THURSDAY	Two miles in 15 minutes or less. Walk 10 minutes. 15 x 150 yards acceleration runs.
FRIDAY	Rest or makeup day.

FOURTH WEEK

| SATURDAY | Milers: 3 x 880 yards in 2:40 each (80 seconds per 440 yards.) Walk five minutes after each. Half-milers: 4 x 400 yards in 65 seconds. Walk four minutes after each. Both milers and half-milers finish with 10 x 150 yards acceleration runs. |
| SUNDAY | Milers: 30-40 x 110 in 17-18 seconds each. Walk and jog 110 yards after each. Half-milers: 20-30 x 110 in 16-17 seconds. Walk and jog 110 yards after each. |

| MONDAY | Milers: 2 x ¾ mile in 80 seconds per 440 yards or four minutes each. Walk 10 minutes after each. |
| | Half-milers: 2 x 660 yards in 1:45-1:50. Walk 10 minutes after each. Both milers and half-milers finish with 10 x 150 yards acceleration runs. |

| TUESDAY | Milers: 10 x 440 yards in 72-74 seconds. Walk two minutes after each. |
| | Half-milers: 6-10 x 220 yards in 30-32 seconds. Walk 220 yards after each. |

WEDNESDAY	Milers: Mile in 5:20-5:30. Walk 10 minutes.
	Half-milers: 880 yards in 2:20-2:25. Walk 10 minutes.
	Both milers and half-milers finish with 20 x 150 yards acceleration sprints.

| THURSDAY | Two miles in 15 minutes or less. Walk 10 minutes. 20 x 150 yards acceleration sprints. |

| FRIDAY | Rest or makeup day. |

Early Competitive Season Training with Two Races per Week

During the competitive racing season there are frequently two races each week, usually on Tuesday and Friday. It is recommended that athletes rest the day prior to competition in the second or third quarter of the season or prior to major competition. Prior to major competition during the latter part of the season, two days rest may be in order, depending upon the individual.

The athlete who runs both the 880 and mile in competition should use the miler's workouts.

| MONDAY | Milers: 10 x 440 yards each in two seconds faster than mile racing pace. Walk and jog two minutes after each. |
| | *Example:* 73 seconds for the five-minute miler. |

Half-milers: 6-8 x 200 yards at racing speed or one second faster than racing speed. Walk and jog two minutes after each.
Example: 34-35 seconds for the 2:20 half-miler.

TUESDAY   Race.

WEDNESDAY   Milers: 30-40 x 110 yards in 16-17 seconds each. Jog and walk 110 yards after each.
Half-milers: 20-30 x 110 yards in 14-16 seconds each, depending upon ability. Jog and walk 110 yards after each.

THURSDAY   Milers and half-milers run 5-8 miles.

FRIDAY   Race.

SATURDAY   Milers: 10 x 440 yards each in two seconds faster than mile racing pace. Walk and jog two minutes after each.
Example: 73 seconds for the five-minute miler.
Half-milers: 6-8 x 200 yards at racing speed or one second faster than racing speed. Walk and jog two minutes after each.
Example: 34-35 seconds for the 2:20 half-miler.

SUNDAY   Milers and half-milers run 5-8 miles.

The Warm Up

Use the same warm up procedure before racing and training. While fully clothed in sweat clothes and flat soled shoes, run one mile continuously in this way: First 440 yards in 3 minutes, second 440 yards in 2.5 minutes, third 440 yards in 2 minutes. For the fourth 440 yards, alternate 50 yards fast and 50 yards slow until the entire 440 is completed. Each of the fast 50-yard runs should be slightly faster than the preceding one with the final one at full speed. Then take 10 minutes for calisthenics and changing to spiked shoes before going directly into the workout. Prior to the race, lie down for 10 minutes in a warm, dry place before appearing at the starting line. At the end of the workout jog one mile in 10 minutes.

Racing Tactics

Even pace running is the most economical way to run. This is especially true in the mile. Ideally, the miler should run his second 880 approximately two to four seconds faster than the first 880. The half-miler usually runs the first 440 two seconds faster than the second.

Certain factors should be considered in deciding upon tactics. These include track conditions (fast, slow, heavy, dry, wet, cut up, curves,) number of competitors, ability of competitors, weather (hot, humid, rain, wind,) personal ability, minimum speed of leading and following, maximum speed of leading and following, etc. A runner takes the lead for the purpose of increasing the pace, decreasing the pace, gaining tactical position and sprinting for the finish. The third quarter of any race is apt to be slowest. A tactical increase in pace during the third one-fourth of a race often proves of great advantage in securing a commanding lead over the opposition. In passing an opponent the runner should make certain he does it quickly and decisively, so that the opponent won't have the chance to fight him off.

A runner should not be afraid to take the pace and lead throughout, or to take the pace from the leader and set his own pace if the opponent does not set a suitable pace. The runner should never lose contact during a race—contact meaning keeping the opponent within effective striking distance wherein he may be caught and passed. This may vary from a few feet to many yards. It is psychologically more difficult to lead than to follow. However, a really good "front runner" has no intention of acting as a pace setter for the rest of the field. His intention is to open a gap, break contact with the field and settle down to fast even-pace running to make certain the opposition does not get within striking distance. A runner should not pass on the turn unless he is sure he will meet no great resistance.

The empirical philosophy behind training has undergone certain changes over the years. Perhaps one of the first was the notion to run very long, slow distances—much longer than the racing distance at much slower than racing speed would mean one could race much faster over a short distance. A man hoping to run a mile in 4:30 might run six to eight miles continuously at a speed of seven or eight minutes per mile. This method generally proved to be false although there is still merit to the occasional long, slow run. For the purpose of a "crash" program, this method definitely will not produce good results. Basically, it is the speed that "hurts" in a race, not the distance.

A second notion, which has been proved highly successful, is to run repeated repetitions of fast runs over short distances at a pace faster than racing speed. According to this concept, if the runner is running at a much faster speed even though it is over a shorter distance, then when he runs the full racing distance at a slower speed he can negotiate the full race at a relatively fast pace.

Long Jump Exercises

Practice the approach run every day. If you are going to jump to the best of your ability you must have an excellent approach.

During the last three to five strides, run on your heels to lower the center of gravity for the thrust upward.

Long jumpers must have strong abdominal muscles. To develop these muscles, exercises such as sit ups, toe touches and leg lifts are helpful.

Weight-lifting exercises—half squats, toe raises, jump ups with weights on the shoulders, curls and straight power lifts—are also important.

Hop with coordinated arm action and short run jump everyday. In this type of jumping concentrate on jumping high and using good technique.

Triple Jump Exercises

Hop on one foot then hop on both feet. Bring your knees up to your chest.

Hop on both feet over a row of hurdles, bringing your knees up to your chest.

Repeat "step" jumps are helpful. Pull the leading leg up toward the chest and jump off one foot and then the other.

Practice the standing triple jump, as well as the approach. Every workout should include a section on running.

Employ the same weight-lifting exercise as for the long jumper.

High Jump Exercises

Practice kicking the right leg as high as possible every day. Valery Brumel of the Soviet Union can touch a basketball rim with his right foot. He has spent much time developing this powerful kick.

Work on the approach run. Gain confidence in your run. Be sure to find proper approach so that in competition you will know exactly where to start the approach.

Do sit ups and push ups every day. You must have strong abdominal muscles to lift your legs.

Practice hopping on one foot and then on the other. Weight-lifting—half squat and toe raise with weights resting on the shoulders—is an excellent way to develop leg power.

Practice lying on a mat on your stomach and then quickly lift your trailing leg up to turn the foot so the toes point upward. This should cause you to roll over onto your back.

Pole Vault Exercises

Find the correct point from which to begin your approach and work on this approach everyday that you practice.

Calisthenics—sit ups, leg lifts, push ups, pull ups, walking on hands, handsprings, rope climbing and continuous hopping—are essential to good conditioning.

Weight-lifting—bicep curl, tripcep pullover and extension, half squat, toe raise, leg lift, dead lift and straight power lift—is most helpful.

Running the hurdles will help you to develop an even stride.

Short run vaulting will help to refine technique. For the beginner short run vaulting is most important for two reasons: **1.** He cannot effectively use the accumulated speed and force of a full run. **2.** He lacks the conditioning which will enable him to take as many full run jumps as he needs.

Practice running with your pole. This can be done by running several 40-yard dashes while carrying the pole.

Shot Put Exercises

The following weight-lifting exercises are very beneficial for shot putters—half squats with the weights on the shoulders, straight power lifts, tricep curls, bicep curls and bench presses.

Also, stand with your legs in the throwing position holding the bar across the chest. Thrust the weights forward and then quickly bring them back to the chest. This exercise is called the *forward thrust.*

The following calisthenics will help develop shot putting ability—push ups, sit ups, half squats and toe raises.

Run short sprints every day as well as practice the circle glide.

Discus Throw Exercises

Weight-lifting—bench press, half squat, dead lift, two-arm curl, one-arm curl, dumbbell flying motion, prone position toe raise, bent arm pullover, twisting with weights on the shoulders and straight arm pullover—helps develop power.

Calisthenics—push ups on fingertips, chin ups, squeezing a rubber ball, sit ups, toe raises, half squats—aid conditioning.

Put a strap on a discus which will hold it to the hand and practice the turn without releasing the discus. This enables you to take many practice turns without tiring the arm.

Running develops leg strength and aids in the development of reaction time. Run each practice.

Javelin Exercises

Practice taking fast cross steps over a 50-yard distance.

Practice throwing a small ball as far as possible using correct javelin form.

Throw a volleyball up in front of you, jump forward to your left foot and catch the ball by slapping down on the ball with your right hand. Throw a heavy medicine ball with an overhead motion.

Put your right arm in a throwing position and have a partner pull back on the arms as you pull forward. Use your body to pull.

Calisthenics—push ups, finger push ups, pull ups, leg lifts—are good conditioners.

Weight-lifting—erect twist, pullover, bench press, jump squat, half squat, pull up and press snatch, forward raise, lateral arm raise and clean and jerk—increases stamina and power.

glossary of track and field terms

A.A.U.: Amateur Athletic Union.

ANCHOR: The final or fourth leg of a relay.

ANGLE OF DELIVERY: Angle to the ground at which an implement is released.

APPROACH: The run and/or adjustments made by the participant prior to the actual competitve effort.

BALL-HEEL-BALL: Method in which distance runners touch the foot to ground while running.

BARRIER: A term used for a hurdle.

BATON: A tube-like object of wood or metal which is passed from one runner to another in a relay race.

BLIND PASS: A relay pass with the outgoing runner receiving the baton without turning his head to look at the approaching runner.

BOX: The container in which a pole vaulter plants the tip of his pole before taking off.

BREAK: Leaving the starting blocks before the gun sounds.

CALISTHENICS: Simple exercises done to warm up and prepare the body for activity.

CHUTE: The prolongation of the straightaway of an oval or semi-oval track.

CIRCLE: Competitive area for the shot, discus, and hammer.

CLOSED POSITION: A powerful throwing position for shot and discus men in which the right shoulder and hip are back.

CROSSBAR: The bar, which can be raised or lowered, placed between two standards for high jump or pole vault.

CUT-DOWN: The dropping of the lead leg when clearing the hurdle.

DRIVE-LEG: The leg exerting the force during stride or take off.

FALSE START: Leaving the starting line before the starting signal is given.

FIELD: Area of participation, as contrasted with the running track.

FLYAWAY: Act of leaving the pole at the height of a vault.

FOLLOW THROUGH: The movement of a part or parts of the body following movement.

FOUL: A competitive effort wasted due to an infraction of a rule.

FRONT CROSS: Finnish method of getting the body into position for javelin throwing.

FRONT RUNNER: One who can run well leading and setting pace.

GRIP: Hand hold on an implement for a competitive event.

HAND OFF: The passing of the baton from the incoming runner to the outgoing runner in a relay.

HEAD WIND: Wind blowing toward the athlete.

HIGH JUMP STANDARDS: Uprights which are used to hold the crossbar for the high jump.

I.C.A.A.A.A.: Intercollegiate Association of Amateur Athletics of America.

INTERCOLLEGIATE COMPETITION: Competition between institutions at the college level.

INTERSCHOLASTIC COMPETITION: Competition between institutions on the secondary school level.

JOGGING: Running at a slow pace.

KICK: Leg speed used at end of a race.

KICKER: Runner who depends upon kick to win.

LEAD LEG: The first leg to leave the ground in jumping. The first leg over the hurdle.

LEAD OFF: The first runner on a relay team.

LEG: A section of a relay. The distance run by a member of a team.

MARKS: An athlete's starting point for a race.

MEDLEY: A relay race in which the various "legs" are of unequal distance.

N.C.A.A.: National Collegiate Athletic Association.

N.F.S.H.S.A.A.: National Federation of State High School Athletic Associations.

PACE: The rate of covering ground while running.

PASSER: The relay runner who "hands off" the baton.

PASSING: Not taking one's jump or vault as it comes up.

PASSING ZONE: A zone in which a pass must be made during a relay.

PIT: An area filled with sawdust, sand or synthetic material in which a long jumper, high jumper or pole vaulter lands.

PULL UP: Raising by pulling of the body in pole vaulting.

PURSUIT RELAY: A relay in which all runners run in the same direction.

PUSH OFF: Pushing up and away from the vaulting pole at the top of the vault.

RECEIVER: The person receiving the baton in a relay race.

RECOVERY LEG: The nondriving leg during running.

REFLEX: Automatic and involuntary muscle reaction.

REVERSE: The follow through after a put or throw.

RHYTHM: Uniform, well coordinated running action.

SAILING: The body in suspension when crossing the hurdle.

SCISSORS JUMP: A method of high jumping in which the legs are moved as if opening and closing a scissors when crossing the bar.

SCRATCH LINE: The take off line which cannot be crossed in the throwing and some jumping events.

SHIFT: Moving the vaulting pole from the carry position into the vaulting box.

SHOT: Iron or brass spheres, 8, 12 or 16 pounds in weight, used for competition.

SHUTTLE RELAY: A relay where the legs are run back and forth over the same course. Half of each relay team are at opposite ends of the prescribed distance.

SPRING: Bounce or lightness of foot.

STANCE: Particular starting position of an athlete.

STANDARDS: Upright objects used to hold crossbars during jumping or vaulting contests.

STARTING BLOCKS: Equipment used by runners to obtain a reliable and firm support for a fast start.

STRADDLE ROLL: A method of high jumping by clearing the bar face down.

STRAIGHTAWAY: Straight area of the track from one curve to the next.

STRIDE: The distance covered by a leg cycle while running.

SWING: Pendulum action of the body or a part of the body.

TAKE OFF: Act of leaving ground as in hurdles, jump or vault.

TAKE OFF FOOT: Foot which drives athlete from the ground.

TAKE OFF MARK: Spot at which athlete leaves the ground.

TECHNIQUE: Form used to execute an action.

TOE BOARD: A restraining board for certain field events, such as the shot put and discus throw.

TOUCH OFF OR TAG: Touching a relay runner rather than passing a baton, as in shuttle races.

WARM UP: Gradual process of raising the body temperature and loosening up muscles prior to strenuous exercise or competition.

WESTERN ROLL: Method of high jumping. Clearing the bar on the side or back.

WIND SPRINT: Practice sprint for conditioning purposes.